The big hit

Story by Jenny Giles
Illustrations by Betty Greenhatch

"Look, Dad!" shouted Jack.

"I can hit the ball

up into the sky."

"Good hit, Jack!" said Dad.

"I can hit the ball,"
said Billy.

"No, Billy," said Jack.
"You are too little."

Dad said, "Here, Billy!
You can kick this big ball
to me.
You are good at kicking."

"No," said Billy.
"I can hit the little ball
like Jack."

Jack said,

"Here is the paddle, Billy."

Dad said,

"Here comes the ball."

"Oh, no!" said Billy.

"Look at the ball, Billy,"
said Jack.
"You can hit it."

"Here it comes," said Dad.

Billy looked at the ball,
and he **hit** it!

"I hit the ball
up to the sky!"
shouted Billy.

"Good hit, Billy!"

said Jack and Dad.